Getting Along
with Your Parents

LIFE ON THE EDGE SERIES

Getting Along
with Your Parents

Dr. James Dobson

WORD PUBLISHING

NASHVILLE

A Thomas Nelson Company

GETTING ALONG WITH YOUR PARENTS

PUBLISHED BY WORD PUBLISHING, NASHVILLE, TENNESSEE.

Scripture quotations used in this book are from The Holy Bible, New International Version (NIV). Copyright © 1973, 1978, 1984, International Bible Society. Used by permission of Zondervan Bible Publishers.

LIBRARY OF CONGRESS CATALOGING-IN-PUBLICATION DATA

Dobson, James C., 1936–
    Getting along with your parents / by James Dobson.
      p. cm. — (Life on the edge series)
    ISBN 0-8499-4232-2
    1. Parent and teenager. 2. Parent and teenager—Religious aspects. 3. Parent and adult child. 4. Teenagers—Family relationships. 5. Young adults—Family relationships. I. Title.
HQ799.15 .D64 2001
306.874—dc21
                                               00-049973
                                                    CIP

Printed in the United States of America.

00 01 02 03 04 05 PHX 9 8 7 6 5 4 3 2 1

Preface

IF YOU ARE BETWEEN SIXTEEN AND TWENTY-SIX years of age, this series of books is written specifically for you. Others are welcome to read along with us, of course, but the ideas are aimed directly at those moving through what we will call the "critical decade."

Some of the most dramatic and permanent changes in life usually occur during those ten short years. A person is transformed from a kid who's still living at home and eating at the parents' table to a full-fledged adult who should be earning a living and taking complete charge of his or her life. Most of the decisions that will shape the next fifty years will be made in this era, including the choice of an occupation, perhaps the decision to marry, and the establishment of values and principles by which life will be governed.

I recall pondering these questions in my youth and thinking how helpful it would be to talk with someone who had a few answers—someone who understood what I was facing. But like most of my friends, I never asked for help.

What makes this period even more significant is the impact of early mistakes and errors in judgment. They can undermine all that is to follow. A bricklayer knows he must be very careful to get his foundation absolutely straight; any wobble in the bricks at the bottom will create an even greater tilt as the wall goes up. So it is in life.

In this series of books, we'll talk about how to interpret the will of God and recognize His purposes for you, the task of thinking through the challenges you are facing, and how you will accomplish your life goals. A contractor would never begin a skyscraper without detailed architectural and engineering plans to guide his or her work. Likewise, persons in the critical decade between age sixteen and twenty-six owe it to their future to figure out who they are and what they want out of life. Helping you do that is what this book is all about.

—Dr. James Dobson

Introduction

THERE COMES A TIME IN A BIRD'S LIFE WHEN HE needs to leave the safe, secure environment of the family nest and fly solo. The bird leaves behind a place where he never had to worry about where his next meal came from and his parents always provided plenty of warmth and comfort. Yet, if the young bird is going to survive he needs to leave the nest behind and set out on his own and learn to take care of himself.

This freedom does not come easily. The young bird will probably make some good decisions and some bad ones, too. He will experience times of great fright and danger and times of excitement and triumph.

In many ways, you will go through the same process. The next several years are a time of leaving the safe haven of your home and spreading your wings. They are a time of adventure and a time of new responsibilities.

But as you spread your wings, there will be inevitable conflict. There will be times when you feel you are ready to fly solo, and your parents will say you're not ready. There will be times when you feel you have made a good decision, and your parents will think otherwise. But despite these conflicts, keeping a good relationship with your parents is important, to both your present happiness and your future.

In *Getting Along with Your Parents,* Dr. James Dobson describes the many times your relationship with your parents will change — as they grow older and you become a friend, then possibly a parent yourself, and eventually more like their parent as you begin assuming more responsibility for their care.

Leaving the nest is never easy, but in the following pages, Dr. Dobson will show you how a good relationship with your parents will help you to soar once you reach the young adult years.

Contents

1 Your Parents Vs. You

A VITALLY IMPORTANT TOPIC DURING THE CRITICAL decade is the relationship between you and your parents. As I'm sure you've observed, the teen years can take a family to the brink of civil war. They can be awful! The battles often begin as early as thirteen years of age and reach their greatest intensity at about eighteen. For some, fighting is still occurring in the twenties, and it inflicts terrible pain on both generations. Whether the conflict comes early or late, nothing else in life can match this era for its ability to alienate people who honestly love and need each other.

At least, that's the way family life often plays out today. I'm sure there has always been friction between parents and children, but the nature of it has changed radically. The culture that once was supportive and respectful of parents has now become the worst enemy of the family. Let me illustrate.

The artistic creations produced by a society at a

given time don't spring from a vacuum. They reflect the opinions and beliefs commonly held by its people. That being true, we can measure change in attitudes by looking at the evolution of music that has occurred in recent years. Let's go back to 1953 when the most popular song in the United States was sung by Eddie Fisher and was titled "Oh, My Papa." Here's a portion of the lyrics:

Oh, my papa, to me he was so wonderful
Oh, my papa, to me he was so good.
No one could be so gentle and so lovable,
Oh, my papa, he always understood.
Gone are the days when he would take me on his knee
And with a smile he'd change my tears to laughter.
Oh, my papa, so funny and adorable,
Always the clown, so funny in his way,
Oh, my papa, to me he was so wonderful
Deep in my heart I miss him so today,
Oh, my papa. Oh, my papa.[1]

That sentimental song accurately reflected the way many people felt about their fathers at that time in our history. Oh sure, there were conflicts and disagreements, but family was family. When it was all said and done, parents were entitled to respect and loyalty, and they usually received it from their children.

THAT WAS THEN . . . THIS IS NOW

By the time I had reached college age, things were starting to change. The subject of conflict between parents and teenagers began to appear as a common theme in artistic creations. The movie *Rebel without a Cause* featured a screen idol named James Dean who seethed with anger at his "Old Man." Marlon Brando starred in *The Wild One,* another movie with rebellion as its theme. Rock-'n'-roll music portrayed it, too.

> *Some early rock-'n'-roll lyrics mixed rebellious messages with humor.*

Some early rock-'n'-roll lyrics mixed rebellious messages with humor, such as a number-one hit from 1958 called "Yakkety-Yak (Don't Talk Back)."[2] But what began as musical humor turned decidedly bitter in the late sixties. Everyone in those days was talking about the "generation gap" that had erupted between young people and their parents. Teenagers and college students vowed they'd never again trust anyone over thirty, and their anger toward parents began to percolate. The Doors released a song in 1968 entitled "The End," in which Jim Morrison fanaticized about killing his father. It concludes with gunshots followed by horrible grunts and groans.[3]

BUT WAIT! IT GETS WORSE

In 1984, Twisted Sister released "We're Not Gonna Take It," which refers to a father as a "disgusting slob" who was "worthless and weak."[4] Then he was blasted out the window of a second-story apartment. This theme of killing parents showed up regularly in the decade that followed. A group called Suicidal Tendencies released a recording in 1983 called "I Saw Your Mommy." Here is an excerpt of the gory lyrics:

> I saw your mommy and your mommy's dead.
> I watched her as she bled,
> Chewed-off toes on her chopped-off feet.
> I took a picture because I thought it was neat.
> I saw your mommy, and your mommy's dead.
> I saw her lying in a pool of red;
> I think it's the greatest thing I'll ever see—
> Your dead mommy lying in front of me.[5]

For sheer banality, nothing yet produced can match "Momma's Gotta Die Tonight," by Ice-T and Body Count.[6] The album sold 500,000 copies and features its wretched lyrics on the CD jacket. Most of them are unfit to quote here, but they involve graphic descriptions of the rapper's mother being

burned in her bed, then beaten to death with a base-
ball bat she had given him as a present, and finally
the mutilation of the corpse into "little bitty pieces."
What incredible violence! There is not a hint of guilt
or remorse expressed by the rapper while telling us of
this murder. In fact, he calls
his mother a "racist b___h"
and laughs while chanting,
"Burn, Mama, burn." My
point is that the most popular music of our culture went
from the inspiration of "Oh,
My Papa" to the horrors of
"Momma's Gotta Die
Tonight" in scarcely more
than a generation. And we have to wonder, where do
we go from here?

> *There is not a
> hint of guilt or
> remorse
> expressed by the
> rapper while
> telling us of this
> murder.*

BOMBARDED BY ANTIFAMILY RHETORIC

One thing is certain: Your generation has been bom-
barded with more antifamily rhetoric than any that
preceded it. When added to equally disturbing messages about drug usage, sex, and violence against
women, the impact has to be considered formidable.
Remember that teenagers (and preteens) do not just
hear such lyrics once or twice. The words are burned
into their minds. They are memorized, sung, and

quoted. And the rock stars who perform them become idols to many impressionable teenagers.

MTV, which promotes the worst stuff available, is telecast into 231,000,000 households in seventy-five countries, more than any other cable program.[7]

Though it will not be popular for me to say it, I believe many of the problems that plague your generation can be traced to this venom pumped into its veins by the entertainment industry in general.

> *Your generation has been bombarded with more antifamily rhetoric than any that preceded it.*

Although I never identified with those who hated their parents, there were times when I thought my folks were "yakety-yaking" too much. I remember working with my father one day when I was fifteen years old. We were cutting the grass and cleaning the garage on a very hot day. For some reason, Dad was particularly cranky that afternoon. He crabbed at me for everything I did, even when I hustled. Finally, he yelled at me for something petty, and that did it. I threw down my rake and quit.

Defiantly, I walked across our property and down the street while my dad demanded that I come back. It was one of the few times I ever took him on like that! I meandered around town for a while, wondering what would happen when I finally went home. Then I strolled over to my cousin's house on the other side of town. That night, I admitted to his father that I'd had a bad fight with my dad and he didn't know where I was. My uncle persuaded me to call home and assure my parents that I was safe. With knees quaking, I phoned my dad.

"Stay there," he said. "I'm coming over."

To say that I was scared would be an understatement. In a short time Dad arrived and asked to see me alone.

"Bo," he began, "I didn't treat you right this afternoon. I was riding your back for no good reason, and I want you to know I'm sorry. Your mom and I want you to come on home now."

He made a friend for life.

Not all family fights end so lovingly, of course. In fact, I'll bet you've been through some tough moments of your own. How about it? Have you had royal shootouts with your mom and dad? Do you harbor deep resentment for things they've said or done? Have you wounded them by your defiance and independence? Are there scars on your relationship that you wish weren't there? Why does it have to be that way?

Admittedly, some of those to whom I am writing have been abused by their parents and their anger is rooted in that pain. But let's assume you are not one of them. Your mother and father love you like crazy and would endure any sacrifice to give you what you need. Why, then, are there such strong negative feelings between you? Let's take a moment to examine the causes of family feuds and offer a few suggestions for improvement.

2 | Everyone Seeks POWER!

THE BASIC SOURCE OF CONFLICT BETWEEN generations is that old bugaboo of power. It is defined as control—control of others, control of our circumstances, and especially control of ourselves. The lust for it lies deep within the human spirit. We all want to be the boss, and that impulse begins very early in life. Studies show that one-day-old infants actually "reach" for control of the adults around them. Even at that tender age, they behave in ways designed to get their guardians to meet their needs.

The desire for power is apparent when a toddler runs from his mother in a supermarket or when a ten-year-old refuses to do his or her homework or when a husband and wife fight over money. We see it when an elderly woman refuses to move to a nursing home. The common thread between these examples is the passion to run our own lives—and everything else if given the chance. People vary in the intensity of this urge, but it seems to motivate all of us to one degree or another.

The grab for control is what produces most of the conflict between parents and teenagers. Many adolescents are not willing to wait for a gradual transfer of power as they develop in maturity, responsibility, and experience. They want to run things now. And often, they insist on sampling the adult vices that have been denied them.

Teenagers vary tremendously in their degree of maturity.

Mothers and fathers face a terrible dilemma when this occurs. They must continue to lead their underaged kids. That is their God-given responsibility as parents—and, it's the law of the land. But parents are limited in what they can force their kids to do. Furthermore, teenagers vary tremendously in their degree of maturity. Some sixteen-year-olds could handle independence and freedom. Others lacking supervision would wreck their lives in a matter of weeks. That sets up a terrible struggle that leaves everyone exhausted, hurt, and angry.

There are some approaches that have been successful in lessening this conflict. The religious group known as the Amish have developed a unique tradition that has succeeded for them. Their children are kept under very tight control when they are young. Strict discipline and harsh standards of behavior are imposed from infancy. When children turn sixteen years of age, however, they enter a period called *Rumspringa*. Suddenly, all restrictions are lifted. They are free to drink, smoke, date, marry, or behave in ways that horrify their parents. Some do just that. But most don't. They are even granted the right to leave the Amish community if they choose. But if they stay, it must be in accordance with the social order. The majority accept the heritage of their families, not because they must, but because they choose to.

Although I admire the Amish and many of their approaches to child-rearing, I believe the Rumspringa concept is implemented too quickly for children raised in a more open society. To take a teenager overnight from rigid control to complete emancipation is an invitation to anarchy. It works in the controlled environment of Amish country, but it is usually disastrous for the rest of us. I've seen families grant "instant adulthood" to their adolescents, to their regret. The result has been similar to what occurred in African colonies when European leadership was suddenly withdrawn. Bloody revolutions were often fought in the power vacuum that was created.

THE TRANSFER OF POWER

If it doesn't work to transfer power suddenly to young people, how can they be established as full-fledged adults without creating a civil war in the process? I have recommended to your parents that they begin granting independence literally in toddlerhood. When a child can tie his shoes, he should be permitted—yes, required—to do it. When she can choose her clothes, she should make her own selections within reason. When he can walk safely to school, he should be allowed to do so. Each year, more responsibility and freedom (they are companions) must be given to the child so that the final release in early adulthood is merely a small, final release of authority. This is the theory, at least. Pulling it off is sometimes quite another matter.

To take a teenager overnight from rigid control to complete emancipation is an invitation to anarchy.

For those of you who are critical of how your mom and dad have handled the transfer of power, I urge you to be charitable to them. It is extremely difficult to be good parents today. Even those who are highly motivated to do the job right often make a mess of things.

Why? Because children are infinitely complex. There is no formula that works in every case. In fact, I believe it is more difficult to raise children now than ever before. Be assured that you will not do the job perfectly, either. Someday, if you are blessed with children, one or more of them will blame you for your failures, just as you may have criticized your parents.

If there is tension within your family today, there are some things you can do to lessen it. The first is to leave home before you overstay your welcome. Many young adults in their early twenties hang around the house too long because they don't know what to do next. That is a recipe for trouble. Your mother and father can't help "parenting" you if you remain under their noses. To them, it seems like only yesterday since you were born. They find it difficult to think of you as an adult.

The way you live probably irritates them, too. They hate your messy room, which would require a tetanus shot just to walk through. They don't like your music. They go to bed early and arise with the sun; you keep the same hours as hamsters. You drive the family car like you've been to Kamikaze Driving School. They want you to get a job—go to school— do *something*. Every day brings a new argument—a new battle. When things deteriorate to that point, it's time to pack.

3   When Is It Time to Leave?

I VISITED A HOME SEVERAL YEARS AGO WHERE this battle was raging. The parents had posted a notice on the refrigerator that summed up their frustration. It said:

Their kids didn't take the hint. They were still there, watching daytime television and arguing over whose turn it was to take out the trash.

The issue of when to leave home is of great importance to your future. Remaining too long under the "parentos" roof is not unlike an unborn baby who refuses to leave the womb. He has every reason to stay awhile. It is warm and cozy there. All his needs are met in that stress-free environment. He doesn't have to work or study or discipline himself.

Until you cut the umbilical cord and begin providing for yourself, you will remain in a state of arrested development.

But it would be crazy to stay beyond the nine months God intended. He can't grow and learn without leaving the security of that place. His development will be arrested until he enters the cold world and takes a few whacks on his behind. It is to everyone's advantage, and especially to the welfare of his mother, that he slide on down the birth canal and get on with life.

So it is in young adulthood. Until you cut the umbilical cord and begin providing for yourself, you will remain in a state of arrested development.

The Scripture hints at this need to press on. The apostle Paul wrote, "When I was a child, I talked like a child, I thought like a child, I reasoned like a child. When I became a man, I put childish ways behind me" (1 Cor. 13:11). Remaining at home with Mom and Dad is the perpetuation of childhood. It may be time to put it behind you.

There is a variation on this theme that is even more problematical. It occurs when you have been away to attend college or to work, and then you've returned to live at home again. That is called "the elastic nest," and it can be a disaster. Why? Because you've been on your own—you've made your own decisions and controlled your own life. You've changed dramatically during your time away, but you return to find that your parents have not. They are just like you left them. They want to tell you how to run your life—what to eat, what to wear, which friends to cultivate, etc. It is a formula for combat.

I understand that situation because I've been through it. My parents handled me wisely in my late teen years, and it was rare for them to stumble into common parental mistakes. That is, however, exactly what happened when I was nineteen years old. We had been a very close-knit family, and it was difficult for my mother to shift gears when I graduated from high school.

During that summer, I traveled 1,500 miles from home and entered a college in California. I will never forget the exhilarating feeling of freedom that swept over me that fall. It was not that I wanted to do anything evil or forbidden. It was simply that I felt accountable for my own life and did not have to explain my actions to anyone. It was like a fresh, cool breeze on a spring morning. Young adults who have not been properly prepared for that moment sometimes go berserk, but I did not. I did, however, quickly become addicted to that freedom and was not about to give it up.

> *Before you criticize your parents for their failures and mistakes, ask yourself: "Will I really do that much better with my own children?" The job is tougher than it looks, and mistakes are inevitable!*
>
> *Thirty-eight Values to Live By*
> —Dr. James Dobson

The following summer, I came home to visit my folks. Immediately, I found myself in conflict with my mom. She was not intentionally insulting. She simply responded as she had done a year earlier when I was still in high school. But by then, I had journeyed down the road toward independence. She was asking me what time I would be coming in at night and urging me to drive the car safely and advising me about what I ate. No offense was intended. My mother had just failed to notice that I had changed and she needed to get with the new program.

Finally, there was a flurry of words between us, and I left the house in a huff. A friend came by to pick me up, and I talked about my feelings as we rode in the car. "Darn it, Bill!" I said. "I don't need a mother anymore."

Then a wave of guilt swept over me. It was as though I had said, "I don't love my mother anymore." I meant no such thing. What I was feeling was a desire to be friends with my parents instead of accepting their authority over me. Freedom was granted very quickly thereafter.

I hope you will be a bit more patient with your parents than I was with mine. I was only nineteen years old, and I wanted it all. I should have given them another year to adjust. Your mom and dad will also change their thinking if you give them a little time. In the meanwhile, if you are twenty-two or older and have been away from home, I would suggest that you not plan to return except for a specified period and unless you have an unusually harmonious relationship with your parents. For most young people, bouncing back is built for trouble.

4   Parenting Is Like . . .

TO GIVE YOU A BETTER PERSPECTIVE ON WHAT your parents might be feeling today, consider this analogy: The task of raising kids is rather like trying to fly a kite on a day when the wind doesn't blow. Mom and Dad run down the road pulling the cute little device at the end of a string. It bounces along the ground and shows no inclination of flying.

Eventually and with much effort, they manage to get it fifteen feet in the air, but great danger suddenly looms. The kite dives toward electrical lines and twirls near trees. It is a scary moment. Will they ever get it safely on its way? Then, unexpectedly, a gust of wind catches the kite, and it sails upward while Mom and Dad feed out line as rapidly as they can.

The kite begins pulling the string, making it difficult to hold on. Inevitably, they reach the end of their line. What should they do now? The kite is demanding more freedom. It wants to go higher. Dad stands on his tiptoes and raises his hand to accommodate the tug. It is now grasped tenuously between his index finger and thumb, held upward toward the sky. Then the moment of release comes. The string slips through his fingers, and the kite soars majestically into God's beautiful sky.

Mom and Dad stand gazing at their precious "baby," who is now gleaming in the sun, a mere pinpoint of color on the horizon. They are proud of what they've done—but sad to realize that their job is finished. It was a labor of love. But where did the years go?

> *The task of raising kids is rather like trying to fly a kite on a day when the wind doesn't blow.*

Not only is it healthy to understand what your parents are thinking during this "letting-go" period, but I think you should also know what the future holds between you and them. The natural progression during a lifetime moves from authority in childhood to friendship during your adult years and finally to your parents' dependency on you as they age. Can you believe that? Those strong people on whom you have leaned will, if they live long enough, look to you eventually for strength and leadership. It is one of the most dramatic turnarounds that occurs in this human experience.

EVENTUALLY, THE ROLES WILL CHANGE

Writer and humorist Erma Bombeck described that transformation in her book *If Life Is a Bowl of Cherries, What Am I Doing in the Pits?* Included in that collection of writings is a short piece entitled "When Does the Mother Become the Daughter and the Daughter Become the Mother?" Erma begins by saying that her mother had always been strong, independent, and secure. She had attempted to model herself after this woman who had brought her into the world. But in recent years, Mom was changing. She was undeniably becoming more childlike.

> *They are proud of what they've done—but sad to realize that their job is finished.*

Erma first noticed the change when they were riding in a car one day. She was driving and her mom was sitting near the right front door. Suddenly an emergency occurred, causing Erma to slam on the brakes. Instinctively, she reached out to keep her mother from hitting the windshield. When the crisis had passed, the two women sat looking at one another. Each realized that something had changed in their relationship . . . for in prior years, Mom would have attempted to protect Erma.

Take in a great breath of air and then blow it out. Contained in that single breath were at least three nitrogen atoms that were breathed by every human being who ever lived, including Jesus Christ, William Shakespeare, Winston Churchill, and every president of the United States. This illustrates the fact that everything we do affects other people, positively or negatively. That's why it is foolish to say, "Do your own thing if it doesn't hurt anybody else." Everything we do affects other people.

Thirty-eight Values to Live By
—Dr. James Dobson

Then there was the following Thanksgiving when Erma baked the turkey and her mother set the table.

Clearly, the mother was becoming the daughter, and the daughter was becoming the mother. As time passed, the transformation became more dramatic. When the two women were going shopping, it was Erma who said, "My goodness, don't you look nice in that new dress," and, "Don't forget to wear your sweater so you won't get cold in the department stores." Echoing in her mind was the advice of a concerned mother, "Button up your coat, Erma. Wear your galoshes, stay warm, take care of yourself."

She didn't want to see this strong, noble woman become dependent— childlike— insecure.

Mrs. Bombeck understood the new role she was asked to play but resisted it vigorously. She didn't want to see this strong, noble woman become dependent— childlike—insecure. Nevertheless, the inexorable march of time could not be resisted. She had to get her mother up at night to take her to the bathroom and to care for most of her physical needs. How different the relationship had become. When Erma was a kindergartner, she had made a plaster-of-Paris "hand" that decorated the kitchen wall. Forty years later, mom was sent to a senior citizens' crafts class where she made a macramé. It eventually hung in her room at the Bombeck home.

As senility began to creep in, Erma found her own frustration rising to a crescendo. She said on one occasion, "Mom, will you please quit talking about seeing Dad last night? You know he's been gone for ten years." But Mom couldn't help it because she was no longer mentally competent. That completed the transformation. The mother had become the daughter, and the daughter had become the mother.

Shortly thereafter, Erma and her own daughter were riding in a car one day. There was a sudden stacking of cars and the illumination of brake lights. Instinctively, the daughter reached out to protect Erma from hitting the windshield. They looked at each other for a moment, and Erma said, "My Lord! How quickly!"[8]

How quickly, indeed! One of the most wrenching experiences of the forties for me was watching my mother become my daughter and begin to look at me as her father. She eventually developed Parkinson's disease and went through the slow decline toward dependency and death. In the end, she was childlike in a way I would not have believed possible a few decades earlier.

5 Be Prepared for Inevitable Change

WHY HAVE I CHOSEN TO SHARE THIS ASPECT OF life with those of you who are young with parents still in the bloom of health? Because it may make you more tolerant now to understand that the power they hold is temporary. You won't always have to struggle to rid yourself of their authority. It will be handed to you. Even five more years will bring remarkable changes in your relationship.

Before you know it, their time will come to leave this world, if the probabilities hold true. You will then be left to carry on without them. And then, would you believe, one day you will become the "son" or "daughter" of your children, and they will become your "parents"?

Let me speak candidly to those of you who have been most angry at your parents. Given the brevity of life and the temporary nature of all human relationships, can you find it within your hearts to forgive them? Perhaps my personal experience will speak to you. My mother closed her eyes for the last time on June 26, 1988, and went to be with the Lord. She had been so vibrant—so important to each member of our family. I couldn't imagine life without her just a few years earlier. But time passed so quickly, and before we knew it, she had grown old and sick and incompetent. This human experience is like that. In just a brief moment, it seems, our fleeting days are gone, and as King David said, "The place thereof will know it no more."

> *Before you know it, their time will come to leave this world.*

As I sat at the memorial service for my good mother, I was flooded with memories and a profound sense of loss. But there was not the slightest hint of regret, remorse, or guilt. There were no hurtful words I wished I could have taken back. There were no brawls—no prolonged conflicts—that remained unresolved between my parents and me.

Why not? Was I a perfect son, born to flawless parents? Of course not. But in 1962, when Shirley and I had been married two years and I was twenty-six years old, I remember saying to her, "Our parents will not always be with us. I see now the incredible

28

brevity of life that will someday take them from us. We must keep that in mind as we live out our daily lives. I want to respond to both sets of parents in such a way that we will have no regrets after they are gone. This is what I believe the Lord wants of us."

To those of you who are in need of this advice, I urge you not to throw away these good, healthy times. Your parents will not always be there for you. Please think about what I have written and be careful not to create bitter memories that will hang above you when the record is in the books. No conflict is worth letting that happen.

I'll leave you with a powerful story by Sue Kidd that will make its own case. I hope you'll read it carefully. There's a message here for all of us:

DON'T LET IT END THIS WAY

The hospital was unusually quiet that bleak January evening, quiet and still like the air before a storm. I stood in the nurses' station on the seventh floor and glanced at the clock. It was 9 P.M.

I threw a stethoscope around my neck and headed for room 712, last room on the hall. Room 712 had a new patient. Mr. Williams. A man all alone. A man strangely silent about his family.

As I entered the room, Mr. Williams looked up eagerly, but dropped his eyes when he saw it was only me, his nurse. I pressed the stethoscope over his chest and listened. Strong, slow, even beating. Just what I wanted to hear. There seemed little indication he had suffered a slight heart attack a few hours earlier.

He looked up from his starched white bed. "Nurse, would you—" He hesitated, tears filling his eyes. Once before he had started to ask me a question, but had changed his mind.

I touched his hand, waiting.

He brushed away a tear. "Would you call my daughter? Tell her I've had a heart attack. A slight one. You see, I live alone and she is the only family I have." His respiration suddenly speeded up.

I turned his nasal oxygen up to eight liters a minute. "Of course I'll call her," I said, studying his face.

He gripped the sheets and pulled himself forward, his face tense with urgency. "Will you call her right away—as soon as you can?" He was breathing fast—too fast.

"I'll call her the very first thing," I said, patting his shoulder.

I flipped off the light. He closed his eyes,

such young blue eyes in his 50-year-old face.

Room 712 was dark except for a faint night light under the sink. Oxygen gurgled in the green tubes above his bed. Reluctant to leave, I moved through the shadowy silence to the window. The panes were cold. Below a foggy mist curled through the hospital parking lot.

"Nurse," he called, "could you get me a pencil and paper?"

I dug a scrap of yellow paper and a pen from my pocket and set it on the bedside table.

I walked back to the nurses' station and sat in a squeaky swivel chair by the phone. Mr. Williams's daughter was listed on his chart as the next of kin. I got her number from information and dialed. Her soft voice answered.

"Janie, this is Sue Kidd, a registered nurse at the hospital. I'm calling about your father. He was admitted tonight with a slight heart attack and—"

"No!" she screamed into the phone, startling me. "He's not dying, is he?"

"His condition is stable at the moment," I said, trying hard to sound convincing.

Silence. I bit my lip.

"You must not let him die!" she said. Her

31

voice was so utterly compelling that my hand trembled on the phone.

"He is getting the very best care."

"But you don't understand," she pleaded. "My daddy and I haven't spoken in almost a year. We had a terrible argument on my 21st birthday, over my boyfriend. I ran out of the house. I—I haven't been back. All these months I've wanted to go to him for forgiveness. The last thing I said to him was, 'I hate you.'"

Her voice cracked and I heard her heave great agonizing sobs. I sat, listening, tears burning my eyes. A father and a daughter, so lost to each other. Then I was thinking of my own father, many miles away. It had been so long since I had said, "I love you."

As Janie struggled to control her tears, I breathed a prayer. "Please God, let this daughter find forgiveness."

"I'm coming. Now! I'll be there in 30 minutes," she said. *Click.* She had hung up.

I tried to busy myself with a stack of charts on the desk. I couldn't concentrate. Room 712; I knew I had to get back to 712. I hurried down the hall nearly in a run. I opened the door.

Mr. Williams lay unmoving. I reached for his pulse. There was none.

"Code 99, Room 712. Code 99. Stat." The alert was shooting through the hospital within seconds after I called the switchboard through the intercom by the bed.

Mr. Williams had had a cardiac arrest.

With lightning speed I leveled the bed and bent over his mouth, breathing air into his lungs. I positioned my hands over his chest and compressed. One, two, three. I tried to count. At fifteen I moved back to his mouth and breathed as deeply as I could. Where was help? Again I compressed and breathed. Compressed and breathed. He could not die!

"O God," I prayed. "His daughter is coming. Don't let it end this way."

The door burst open. Doctors and nurses poured into the room pushing emergency equipment. A doctor took over the manual compression of the heart. A tube was inserted through Mr. Williams's mouth as an airway. Nurses plunged syringes of medicine into the intravenous tubing.

I connected the heart monitor. Nothing. Not a beat. My own heart pounded. "God, don't let it end like this. Not in bitterness and hatred. His daughter is coming. Let her find peace."

"Stand back," cried a doctor. I handed him

the paddles for the electrical shock to the heart. He placed them on Mr. Williams's chest. Over and over we tried. But nothing. No response. Mr. Williams was dead.

A nurse unplugged the oxygen. The gurgling stopped. One by one they left, grim and silent.

How could this happen? How? I stood by his bed, stunned. A cold wind rattled the window, pelting the panes with snow. Outside— everywhere—seemed a bed of blackness, cold and dark. How could I face his daughter?

When I left the room, I saw her against the wall by a water fountain. A doctor who had been inside 712 only moments before stood at her side, talking to her, gripping her elbow. Then he moved on, leaving her slumped against the wall.

Such pathetic hurt reflected from her face. Such wounded eyes. She knew. The doctor had told her that her father was gone.

I took her hand and led her into the nurses' lounge. We sat on little green stools, neither saying a word. She stared straight ahead at a pharmaceutical calendar, glass-faced, almost breakable-looking.

"Janie, I'm so, so sorry," I said. It was piti- fully inadequate.

"I never hated him, you know. I loved him," she said.

God, please help her, I thought.

Suddenly she whirled toward me. "I want to see him."

My first thought was, *Why put yourself through more pain? Seeing him will only make it worse.* But I got up and wrapped my arm around her. We walked slowly down the corridor to 712. Outside the door I squeezed her hand, wishing she would change her mind about going inside. She pushed open the door.

We moved to the bed, huddled together, taking small steps in unison. Janie leaned over the bed and buried her face in the sheets.

I tried not to look at her at this sad, sad good-bye. I backed against the bedside table. My hand fell upon a scrap of yellow paper. I picked it up. It read:

My dearest Janie,

I forgive you. I pray you will also forgive me. I know that you love me.

I love you too.
Daddy

The note was shaking in my hands as I thrust it toward Janie. She read it once. Then twice. Her tormented face grew radiant. Peace began to glisten in her eyes. She hugged the scrap of paper to her breast.

"Thank You, God," I whispered, looking up at the window. A few crystal stars blinked through the blackness. A snowflake hit the window and melted away, gone forever.

Life seemed as fragile as a snowflake on the

The universe and everything in it will someday pass away and be made new by the Creator. Therefore, the events of today that seem so important are not really very significant, except those matters that will survive the end of the universe (such as securing your own salvation and doing the work of the Lord).

Thirty-eight Values to Live By
—Dr. James Dobson

window. But thank You, God, that relationships, sometimes fragile as snowflakes, can be mended together again—but there is not a moment to spare.

I crept from the room and hurried to the phone. I would call my father. I would say, "I love you."[9]

6 Questions from the Edge

1. My dad is going through a big-time midlife crisis. At least that's what my mom says about him. Can you explain this to me? Why is he kind of going crazy at this time?

Well, I'll describe a typical midlife crisis, although every individual is unique and every case is different. The man in this mess is likely to be in his forties, but it could be earlier or later. He has worked very hard all his adult life, but he's become bored with his job. He is keenly aware that he can't afford to quit or take a lower-paying position. Too many people are depending on him—not only his wife and teenage son and daughter, but also his own aging parents, too. His marriage has been unexciting for years, and he's begun wishing he could get out of it.

Another major influence on this man is his age. For the first time in his life, he's noticing that the sand is running out of the hourglass. He realizes that the best years may be behind him and he's going to be old before very long. He begins to feel a kind of panic. Perhaps the best word to describe what this man is feeling is *trapped*. Life is passing him by, and he's stuck in a monotonous existence with no way out.

He wounds his children, tears out his wife's heart, and usually destroys his own life.

Right at that critical moment, a young, exciting woman may come along. She is probably a divorcée who is lonely and has needs of her own. She senses his restlessness and finds it enticing. He is very flattered by the attention she gives him. He feels young and virile when he's with her, and he begins thinking unthinkable thoughts. *Maybe, just maybe* . . . A whole new world beckons him, one filled with lust, freedom, and escape.

I counseled such a man who dumped a wife and four children and resigned from an outstanding job. When I asked him why he did it, he said, "I had given my entire life to others, and quite frankly, fun and games looked good to me."

This description of the turmoil behind a midlife crisis is written from a man's point of view, but I don't want you to misunderstand me. His behavior is not justified, and in fact, it is a disaster for everyone concerned. He wounds his children, tears out his wife's heart, and usually destroys his own life. Because God will not tolerate sinful behavior, the man frequently throws over his faith and charts a new course. He has just made the biggest mistake of his life even though he may not know it yet.

I certainly hope your father is not going down this road. You and the rest of the family need to pray that his eyes will be opened before it is too late. And your mother should read my book *Love Must Be Tough*.

2. My friend is sixteen years old, and she is very rebellious. She got so mad at her parents this year that she ran away from home. I got a letter from her, and she's living on the streets in Hollywood. It sounds like she's doing okay, but I sure wish she'd come home. I don't even know how to contact her or I'd try to talk her into making up with her parents. They're really nice people.

Your friend probably does not realize what an enormous risk she is taking. I saw a report recently that indicated just how dangerous that lifestyle is. It showed that 62 percent of underage girls who live on the streets die before their eighteenth birthday.[10]

Isn't that tragic? They either are murdered, commit suicide, die of disease, or fatally overdose on drugs. I wish every teenager, and especially every teenage girl, knew of the danger lurking in the city. It's better to stay home and try to work things out than to subject themselves to the horrors of an early death.

3. You talked about music and its influence on my generation. It caused a different kind of problem for me. I've been having trouble hearing in one ear, and I went to a doctor to find out why. He put me through a bunch of tests and then told me that I have damaged my hearing by listening to so much loud music—especially when wearing a headset like a Walkman. I've been doing that ever since I was a preschooler, but no one ever told me that that could be damaging. Could you comment on that?

You've learned something rather late that you should have been told when you were younger. Our hearing apparatus is a mechanical instrument, dependent on three little bones in the middle ear. These delicate parts work together to transmit vibrations to the eardrum, where they are then perceived as sound. Like any mechanical device, however, this apparatus is subject to wear. Therefore, those who live in a noisy environment, including those who keep a headset blaring in their ears, are continually operating those delicate parts and are gradually decreasing their hearing acuity.

A study was conducted of natives living in a quiet village within an isolated Amazon rain forest. They rarely heard noises louder than a squawking parrot or

> *The human body seems indestructible when we are young. However, it is incredibly fragile and must be cared for if it is to serve us for a lifetime. Too often, the abuse it takes during early years (from drugs, improper nutrition, sporting injuries, etc.) becomes painful handicaps during later years.*
>
> *Thirty-eight Values to Live By*
> —Dr. James Dobson

the sounds of children laughing and playing. Not surprisingly, their hearing remained almost perfect even into old age. There was virtually no deafness known to the tribe.

By contrast, people living in modern industrial societies are subject to the continual bombardment of noise pollution. Motorcycles, garbage trucks, television, and high-powered machines pound their ears from morning to night. Young people are particularly at risk because of their music. Attending a Rolling Stones concert is equivalent to being strapped to the bottom of a jet airplane that is taking off, or like being tied to the hood of a Mack truck going sixty miles an hour.

Singer Pete Townshend, lead singer of the legendary rock group The Who, is almost totally deaf in one ear from playing for years near electronic amplifiers and huge speakers. He issued a warning to those who like their music loud. Someday, people will regret the unnecessary wear and tear on their hearing mechanism. We only have one body, and we must help it serve us for a lifetime.

Like a ninety-year-old man said, "If I'd have known I was gonna live so long I'd have taken better care of myself."

4. In your house would you ever, under any circumstances, permit your son or daughter to room with a person of the opposite sex without benefit of marriage?

No. That would be dishonoring God and a violation of the moral principles on which Shirley and I have staked our lives. I would bend for my kids, but never that far.

Notes

1. "Oh, My Pa-Pa" (O Mein Papa). English words by John Turner. Music and original lyric by Paul Burkhard. Copyright © 1948, 1950 Musikverlag und Buhnenvertrieb Zurich A.G., Zurich, Switzerland. Copyright © 1953 Shapiro, Bernstein, & Co., Inc., New York. Copyrights renewed. International copyright secured. All rights reserved. Used by permission.

2. The Coasters, "Yakkety-Yak (Don't Talk Back)," © 1953 Atco Records.

3. The Doors, "The End," © 1968 Viva Records.

4. Twisted Sister, "We're Not Gonna Take It," © 1984 Atlantic Records.

5. "I Saw Your Mommy," written by Mike Muir, 1984 American Lesion Music (BMI)/You'll Be Sorry Music. Administered by BUG. All rights reserved. Used by permission.

6. Ice-T and Body Count, "Momma's Gonna Die Tonight," © 1992 Sire Records.

7. Jill Brookes, "Its Empire Stretches Worldwide," *New York Post,* 22 April 1993, 21.

8. Erma Bombeck, *If Life Is a Bowl of Cherries, What Am I Doing in the Pits?* (New York: Random-Fawcett, 1979).

9. Sue Kidd, "Don't Let It End This Way," *Focus on the Family Magazine,* January 1985, 6–7, 11.

10. International Catholic Bureau, Lusanne, Switzerland, 24 March 1994, 15.

PORTIONS OF THIS SERIES OF BOOKS HAVE BEEN previously published in other books by James Dobson. The author is grateful to these publishers for permission to reprint from these volumes:

Thirty-eight Values to Live By, Word Publishing, 2000.

Life on the Edge: A Young Adult's Guide to a Meaningful Future, Word Publishing, 1995.

Dr. Dobson Answers Your Questions, Tyndale House Publishers, 1988.

Emotions: Can You Trust Them? Regal Books, 1984.

Hide or Seek, Fleming H. Revell Company, 1974, 1990.

Love for a Lifetime, Multnomah, 1987.

Love Must Be Tough, Word Publishing, 1983.

Parenting Isn't for Cowards, Word Publishing, 1987.

Preparing for Adolescence, Regal Books, 1980, 1989.

The Strong-Willed Child, Tyndale House Publishers, 1978.

Straight Talk to Men and Their Wives, Word Publishing, 1980.

What Wives Wish Their Husbands Knew about Women, Tyndale House Publishers, 1975.

When God Doesn't Make Sense, Tyndale House Publishers, 1993.

About the Author

DR. JAMES DOBSON is founder and president of Focus on the Family, a non-profit evangelical organization dedicated to the preservation of the home. He is recognized as one of America's foremost authorities on the family and is the author of numerous books, including *The New Dare to Discipline, The Strong-Willed Child, When God Doesn't Make Sense, Love Must Be Tough, Straight Talk to Men, Parenting Isn't for Cowards,* and *Life on the Edge: A Young Adult's Guide to a Meaningful Future.* Dr. Dobson is a licensed psychologist in the state of California and a licensed marriage, family and child therapist in the state of Colorado. He was formerly an assistant professor of pediatrics at the University of Southern California School of Medicine. His international radio broadcast, *Focus on the Family,* is heard on more than four thousand stations worldwide. He and his wife, Shirley, are the parents of two young adult children, Ryan and Danae.

dditional books in the *Life on the Edge* Series:

Adapted from the best-selling book, *Life on the Edge*, these
seven pocket-sized booklets offer insight and advice for a
generation searching for significance. Additional books in
this series cover such topics as:

emotions

love

money

compatibility

God's will

parents

life's ironies

WORD PUBLISHING
www.wordpublishing.com